Sunday is market day,
my favorite day of the week.

Mom and I are getting ready to go.
Together we make a shopping list
of what we'll need for the week.
But we don't just have to stick to
the list, the market is full
of surprises!

PUMPKIN
POTATOES
APPLES
MUSHROOMS
PINEAPPLE
MANGO
EGGS
BREAD
ORANGES
RASPBERR
AVOCADOS
TOMATOES
ONIONS
GINGER
BASIL
FLOWERS

We'll need money to pay for
everything. It's my job to count
out the coins.

Of course we need something
to carry our shopping in. We
gather all our bags. I like to
push the trolley. We're ready —
off we go!

BAGS ON
WHEELS

PAPER BAGS

BOXES

TROPPO BANANAS

Top POTaToes

BASKET

STRING BAG

TOTE BAG

The first stall we visit has piles of potatoes and pumpkins. Each pumpkin has its own magnificent pattern. We choose a big butternut squash to make pumpkin soup — yum!

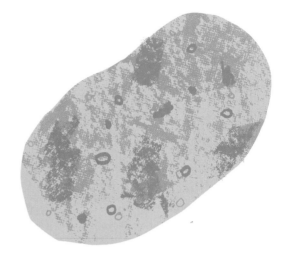

SOME POTATOES ARE COVERED IN DIRT, BUT ALL THEY NEED IS A QUICK SCRUB AND THEY'RE READY TO GO

PUMPKIN
POTATOES
APPLES
MUSHROOMS
PINEAPPLE
MANGO
EGGS
BREAD
ORANGE
RASPBERR
AVO
T

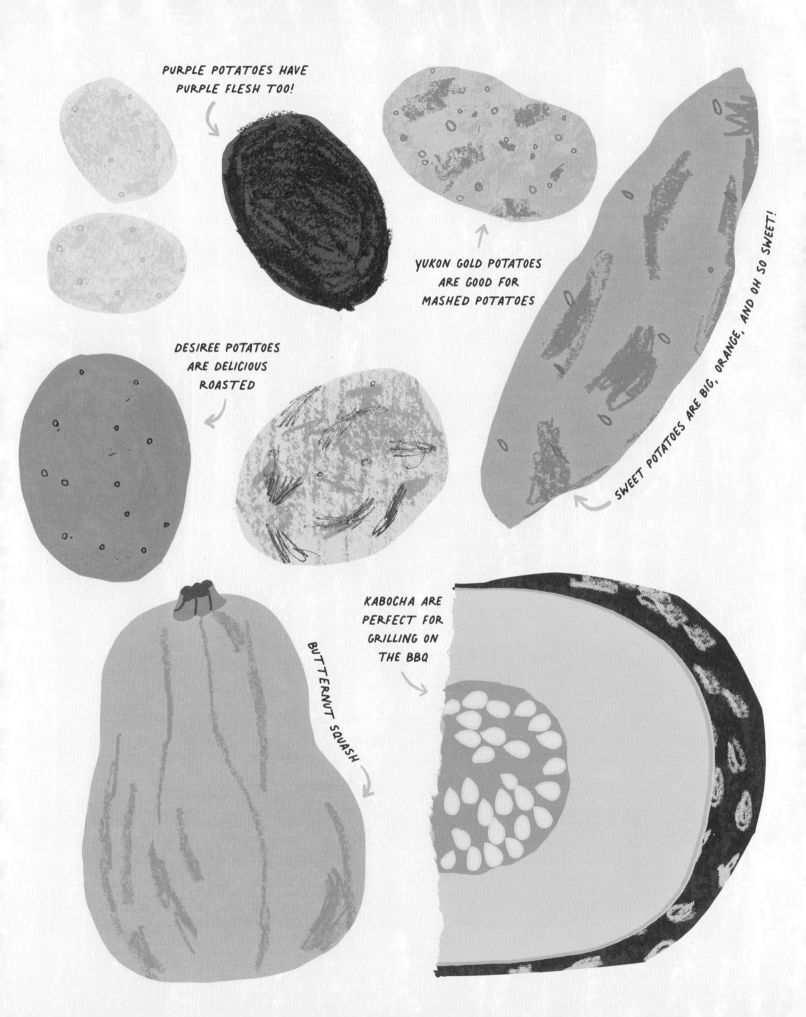

PURPLE POTATOES HAVE PURPLE FLESH TOO!

YUKON GOLD POTATOES ARE GOOD FOR MASHED POTATOES

DESIREE POTATOES ARE DELICIOUS ROASTED

SWEET POTATOES ARE BIG, ORANGE, AND OH SO SWEET!

KABOCHA ARE PERFECT FOR GRILLING ON THE BBQ

BUTTERNUT SQUASH

The next stall is John and Jenny's. It has apples, apples, and more apples. And there are some pears too. Mom fills up our bag because we all love them. She's teaching me the names of all the different varieties. John and Jenny also have bees at their orchard. They make great honey!

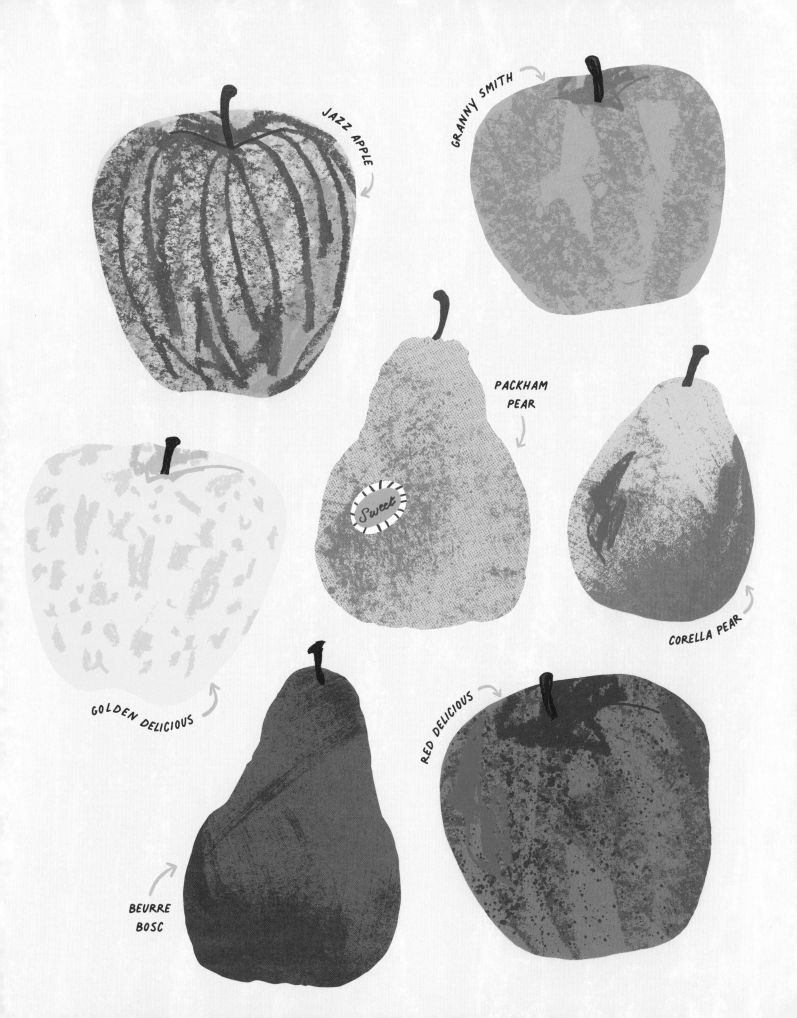

JAZZ APPLE

GRANNY SMITH

PACKHAM PEAR

Sweet

CORELLA PEAR

GOLDEN DELICIOUS

BEURRE BOSC

RED DELICIOUS

We always buy our vegetables at Antonio's stall. He loves to chat! Today he tells me that some vegetables have more than one name. He recommends his big field mushrooms, so we take some of those to try.

SOMETIMES STALL HOLDERS USE SMALL BASKETS LIKE THIS TO WEIGH THE PRODUCE OUT FOR PRICING

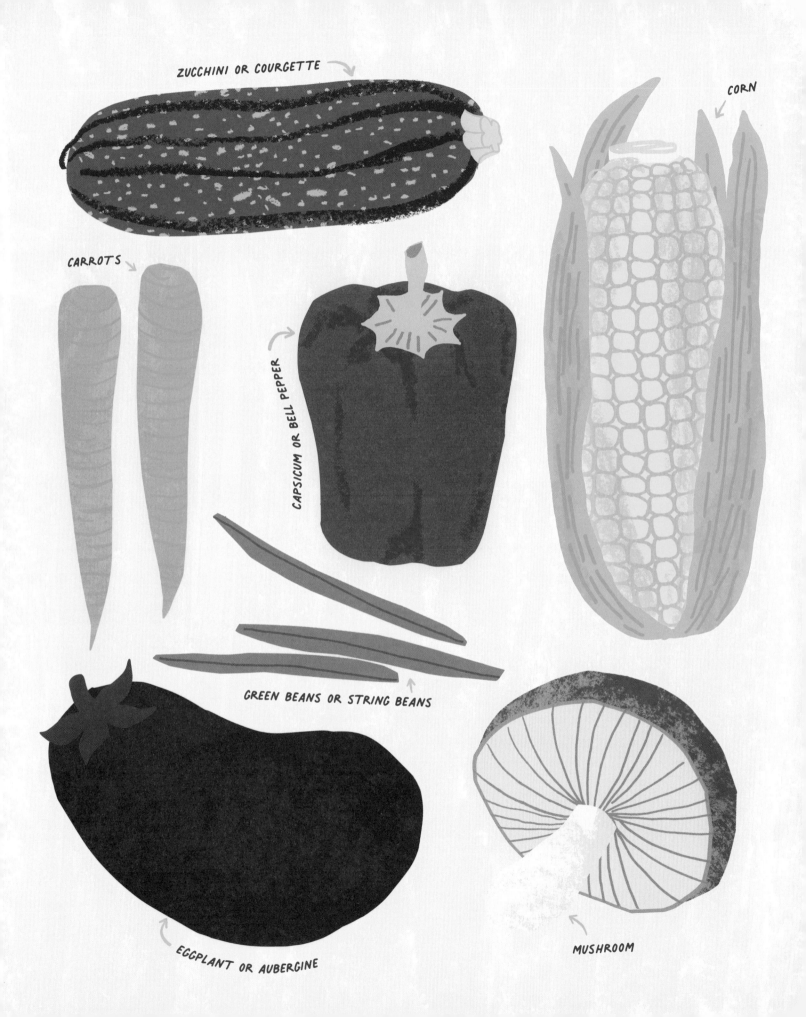

ZUCCHINI OR COURGETTE

CORN

CARROTS

CAPSICUM OR BELL PEPPER

GREEN BEANS OR STRING BEANS

EGGPLANT OR AUBERGINE

MUSHROOM

I love stopping at May's fruit stall because it always looks beautiful. Today she gives me some dragon fruit to try. It's full of little black seeds and tastes a bit sweet. Mom let me choose one special fruit. I pick a big golden pineapple.

"Careful," says May.

"It's spiky!"

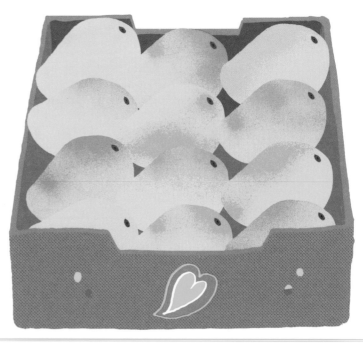

MANGOES HAVE MANY DIFFERENT VARIETIES, INCLUDING KENSINGTON PRIDE, ALPHONSO, AND CALYPSO. THEY GROW ON LARGE EVERGREEN TREES THAT MAKE GREAT SHADE!

PUMPKIN
POTATOES
APPLES
MUSHROOMS
PINEAPPLE
MANGO
EGGS
BREAD
ORANGE
RASPPER
AVO
T

WATER
WH
HAL

CANTALOUPES
Whole / Half

DRAGON FRUIT GROWS ON A CACTUS

PINEAPPLE GROWS OUT OF THE GROUND FROM A LEAFY PLANT

WATERMELON AND CANTALOUPE BOTH GROW FROM VINES THAT CRAWL ALONG THE GROUND

Next we buy our eggs.
The egg man tells us the hens
who laid them live on a farm
two hours away. He checks
our eggs to make sure there
aren't any broken ones, and
Mom puts them into our
basket carefully.

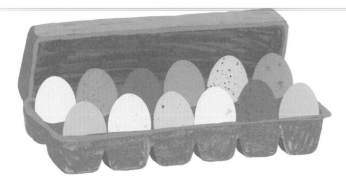

EGGS OFTEN COME IN CARTONS OF A DOZEN, WHICH
IS TWELVE, AND HALF A DOZEN, WHICH IS SIX

DUCK EGGS ARE
SOMETIMES A BEAUTIFUL
PALE-BLUE COLOR

CHICKENS LAY DIFFERENT
COLORED EGGS BUT EACH
CHICKEN WILL LAY
THE SAME COLOR
EVERY TIME

QUAIL EGGS
ARE SPECKLED
AND REALLY
TINY!

GOOSE EGGS ARE ABOUT THE SIZE OF THREE CHICKEN EGGS

FRUIT LOAF

MULTI GRAIN

SEEDED RYE

OLIVE BREAD

A wonderful smell leads us
towards Pierre's bread stall.
He bakes all the bread himself,
and it is always delicious.

Mom asks for today's special
while I give Pierre's dog,
Claude, a pat.

CRUSTY SOURDOUGH WITH SOUP IS A GREAT WINTER MEAL

POPPYSEED BAGELS
— FANTASTIC FOR LUNCHES

FRUIT BREAD MAKES THE MOST DELICIOUS
BREAKFAST — ESPECIALLY WHEN IT'S TOASTED!

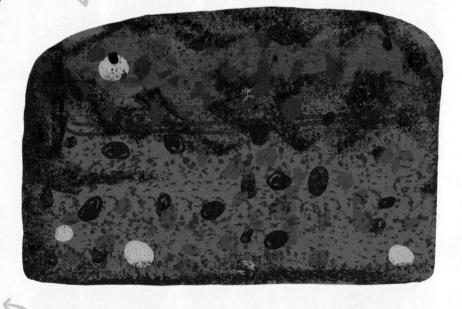

SOFT AND FLUFFY BURGER
BUNS — PERFECT FOR BURGER NIGHT

We stop by Ada's stall to stock up on fruit for my lunch box.

Ada is an expert on what's in season. This week she tells us, "The apricots are just beautiful." Everyone in my family loves stone fruit, so we get lots. They only taste this good when the sun is strong!

STRAWBERRIES ARE OFTEN AVAILABLE ALL YEAR ROUND BUT THE SWEETEST ONES COME IN THE EARLY SUMMER

CHERRIES

APRICOTS

PUMPKIN
POTATOES
APPLES
MUSHROOMS
PINEAPPLE
MANGO
EGGS
BREAD
ORANGE
RASPBERR
AVO
T

ORANGES ARE AVAILABLE ALL
YEAR ROUND, BUT BEST IN
WINTER ALONG WITH THEIR
OTHER CITRUS FRIENDS

PEACHES ARE A MIDSUMMER TREAT

PLUMS ARE THE LAST OF THE
SUMMER STONE FRUITS AND ARE
OFTEN AVAILABLE EVEN PAST SUMMER

APRICOTS HAVE A SEASON THAT IS
SIMILAR TO PEACHES AND NECTARINES
AND ARE BEST IN MIDSUMMER

CHERRIES ARE BEST
IN EARLY SUMMER

BANANAS ARE AVAILABLE ALL YEAR
BUT HAVE TO GROW IN HOT PLACES

Next is Mom's favorite place:
Mike's veggie stall. I've never
seen so many varieties of
lettuce! Mike tells me his trick
for making the best salad: add
some color. "You gotta eat the
rainbow!" he says.

We buy a few avocados —
I love to have them on toast.

AVOCADOS ARE CREAMY AND RICH, GREAT MASHED
FOR GUACAMOLE OR SLICED WITH LEMON ON TOAST

RADISHES HAVE A DELICIOUS PEPPERY TASTE
AND ADD EXTRA CRUNCH TO SALAD

ROMAINE LETTUCE HAS
STRONG LEAVES (THAT DON'T
GO SOGGY AS QUICKLY AS
OTHER TYPES OF LETTUCE),
IT IS GREAT IN BURGERS

BOK CHOY IS PEREFCT IN
A STIR FRY OR ON ITS
OWN AS A SIDE DISH
WITH GARLIC

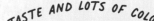

RADICCHIO ADDS A SPECIAL BITTER TASTE AND LOTS OF COLOR TO SALADS

SPINACH IS ONE OF THE
MOST VERSATILE GREENS.
IT CAN BE USED RAW
OR COOKED, AND EVEN IN
SMOOTHIES!

Jan's tomatoes are famous in our family. She has every type — fat ones, thin ones, tiny little cherry tomatoes, and big juicy ones. I love the stripy ones best! We choose a few, and then gently put our collection at the very top of our basket.

CHILIS COME IN ALL SHAPES AND SIZES. AND ALL LEVELS OF HEAT TOO! WATCH OUT!

PUMPKIN
POTATOES
APPLES
MUSHROOMS
PINEAPPLE
MANGO
EGGS
BREAD
ORANGE
RASPBERR
AVOCADO
TOMATOES
ONIONS
GINGER
BASIL
FLOWERS

TRUSS TOMATOES CAN BE
LEFT ON THEIR STEMS AND
ROASTED — THEY
LOOK BEAUTIFUL!

BEEF HEART
TOMATOES HAVE A
RICH FLAVOR THAT
SHINES IN SALADS

ROMA TOMATOES MAKE
THE BEST PASTA SAUCE!

CHERRY TOMATOES
MAKE A PERFECT
SNACK ON THEIR OWN

BLACK TOMATOES TASTE
GREAT AND ADD COLOR TO
YOUR DISHES

SLICER TOMATOES ARE
BEST FOR SANDWICHES
AND BURGERS

Mom loves herbs, so we always go to Yasmin's stall.

Yasmin tells me that herbs make food taste extra special. She always asks us, "So, what are you cooking this week?" and tells us what we'll need.

This is the best-smelling stall. We buy a bunch of basil, coriander, mint, and parsley, and I take a sniff of each one — mmm!

GINGER ADDS A WARMING, SPICY HEAT TO SWEET AND SAVORY DISHES

GARLIC HAS A STRONG, SPICY TASTE THAT IS MOST POWERFUL WHEN IT IS RAW AND MELLOWS WHEN IT COOKS

PUMPKIN
POTATOES
APPLES
MUSHROOMS
PINEAPPLE
MANGO
EGGS
BREAD
ORANGE
RASPBERR
AVOCADO
TOMATOES
ONIONS
GINGER
BASIL
FLOWERS

SHALLOTS ARE SIMILAR TO ONIONS, BUT SMALLER AND SWEETER

CHIVES HAVE AN ONION-Y FLAVOR BUT MILDER AND ARE GREAT CHOPPED IN DRESSINGS WITH SOUR CREAM AND YOGURT

SAGE HAS A STRONG FLAVOR THAT GOES WELL WITH RICH INGREDIENTS LIKE PUMPKIN AND BUTTER

PARSLEY IS ONE OF THE MOST VERSATILE OF HERBS, USED RAW OR COOKED IN MANY DISHES. IT HAS A GRASSY FLAVOR THAT IS SLIGHTLY PEPPERY

THYME HAS SMALL LEAVES ON WOODY STEMS AND AN EARTHY TASTE THAT IS PERFECT FOR CASSEROLES AND SLOW ROASTS

Our last stop is Jamal's flower stall. Buckets of blooms in every color shine in the morning sun. Mom chooses a big bunch of daffodils, and he wraps them in colored tissue paper.

"Ahhh, your mama made the best choice!" Jamal tells me. He says that every week! Mom laughs.

We have everything we need now, and it's time to go home.

PUMPKIN
POTATOES
APPLES
MUSHROOMS
PINEAPPLE
MANGO
EGGS
BREAD
ORANGE
RASPBERR
AVOCADO
TOMATOES
ONIONS
GINGER
BASIL
FLOWERS

LILIES GROW FROM A
BULB AND LAST LONGER
THAN MANY OTHER
FLOWERS IN THE VASE

BANKSIAS GROW
ON LARGE TREES
THAT ARE NATIVE
TO AUSTRALIA

IRISES GROW FROM A BULB
THAT FLOWERS AT THE
SAME TIME EACH YEAR

SUNFLOWERS GROW IN SUMMER FROM
SEEDS, AND CAN BE UP TO 3M TALL!
YOU CAN EAT THE SEEDS

When we get home we unpack
all the bags and baskets.
The table is covered with our shopping.
There's just one thing left to do . . .

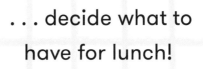

. . . decide what to
have for lunch!

Thank you, market.
See you next week!